EXTREME MACHINES

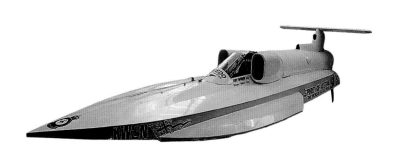

FIRST EDITION
Editor Caroline Bingham; **Art Editor** Helen Melville; **Senior Editor** Linda Esposito
Senior Art Editor Diane Thistlethwaite; **US Editor** Regina Kahney; **Cover Designer** Giles Powell-Smith;
Production Melanie Dowland; **Picture Researcher** Andrea Sadler; **Illustrator** Peter Dennis;
Reading Consultant Linda Gambrell, PhD

THIS EDITION
Editorial Management by Oriel Square
Produced for DK by WonderLab Group LLC
Jennifer Emmett, Erica Green, Kate Hale, *Founders*

Editors Grace Hill Smith, Libby Romero, Michaela Weglinski;
Photography Editors Kelley Miller, Annette Kiesow, Nicole DiMella; **Managing Editor** Rachel Houghton;
Designers Project Design Company; **Researcher** Michelle Harris; **Copy Editor** Lori Merritt;
Indexer Connie Binder; **Proofreader** Larry Shea; **Reading Specialist** Dr. Jennifer Albro;
Curriculum Specialist Elaine Larson

Published in the United States by DK Publishing
1745 Broadway, 20th Floor, New York, NY 10019
Copyright © 2023 Dorling Kindersley Limited
DK, a Division of Penguin Random House LLC
22 23 24 25 26 10 9 8 7 6 5 4 3 2 1
001-333469-May/2023

A catalog record for this book
is available from the Library of Congress.
HC ISBN: 978-0-7440-6844-3
PB ISBN: 978-0-7440-6845-0

DK books are available at special discounts when purchased in bulk for sales promotions, premiums,
fundraising, or educational use. For details, contact: DK Publishing Special Markets,
1745 Broadway, 20th Floor, New York, NY 10019
SpecialSales@dk.com

Printed and bound in China

The publisher would like to thank the following for their kind permission to reproduce their images:
a=above; c=center; b=below; l=left; r=right; t=top; b/g=background

Alamy Stock Photo: dan74 12, Anthony Kay / Flight 44clb, Reuters / Mike Blake 43crb, Haiyin Wang 4-5, 42; **Dreamstime.com:**
VanderWolfImages 18tl; **Guinness World Records Limited:** 20-21b; **Newscom:** Art Seitz / ABACAUSA.COM 26tl; **NOAA:** 22b;
Science Photo Library: NOAA 23; **Shutterstock.com:** Philipe Ancheta 32-33, Corona Borealis Studio 7tr, metamorworks 45;
US Department of Defense: Marine Corps / Lance Cpl. Elias E. Pimentel III 34tl; **Wigetworks:** 43tr

Cover images: *Front:* **123RF.com:** Iakov Kalinin; **Getty Images / iStock:** rancho_runner b; **Shutterstock.com:** pingvin121674 t;
Back: **Shutterstock.com:** Golden Sikorka cla, Vectors Bang cra

All other images © Dorling Kindersley
For more information see: www.dkimages.com

For the curious
www.dk.com

EXTREME MACHINES

Christopher Maynard

CONTENTS

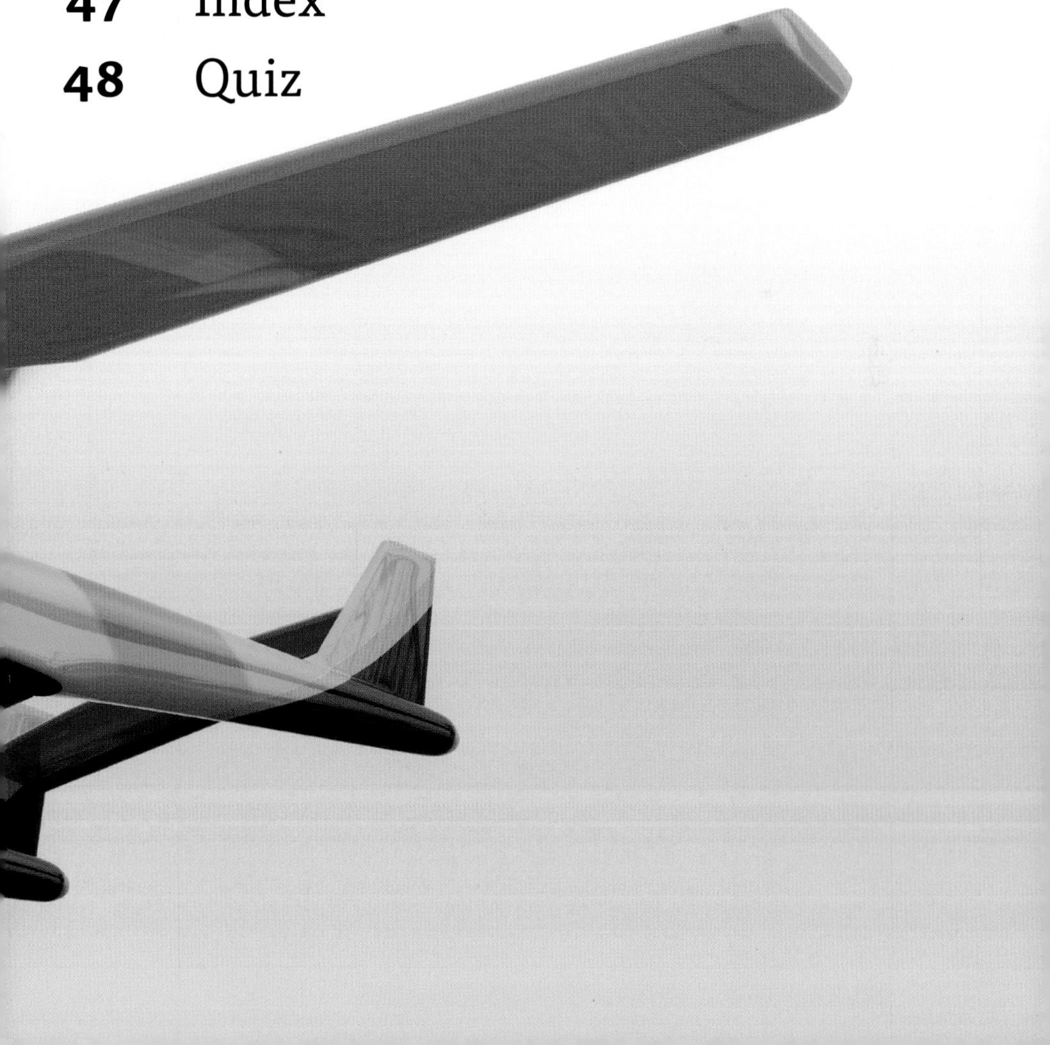

AN EXTREME MACHINE

Most of the cars, boats, and planes we travel in these days are reliable and safe. Most of them are perhaps a little ordinary, too, because we see them every day. But there are a lot of unique machines that do something fantastic. They go ridiculously fast or fly incredibly high.

On the Sea
Offshore powerboats race along more than three times faster than a car is allowed to travel on the highway.

They are extreme machines. Most people would love to have a chance to see them close-up or—even better—ride in them.

In this book, you'll find out what some of the weirdest machines on Earth can do. You'll also find out how they work and how people risk their lives trying to take them to extremes.

Space Tourists
The most powerful rocket ever built, the SpaceX Starship plans to carry 100 passengers at a time to places like the Moon and Mars.

Ray Power
Solar cars are powered by the Sun's rays, not by gasoline. This car, the *Mad Dog*, can reach more than 40 miles per hour (70 kph) (but not on cloudy days!).

No Tread
Slick tires have no treads, or grooves. Treads in car tires let rainwater out so the car doesn't skid.

DRAG-CAR RACING

The two drivers sat in their drag cars waiting for the next quarter-mile (400-m) race. They watched an assistant splash water over both sets of rear tires, or slicks. The fat slicks were now slippery, as the drivers locked their front brakes and revved their gleaming engines. With a roar that set the packed stadium cheering, the slicks began to spin. Clouds of smoke rose behind the drag cars.

In seconds, the rubber slicks turned soft with heat. It gave them a grip on the track that was as sticky as a leech's. There would be no unwanted wheel spin and wasted seconds when the race began, no matter how fast the drivers set off.

Each driver now popped his gear stick into first and gripped the handbrake to hold his car back. Each driver felt the engines begin to tug. Before them was a "Christmas tree" of lights, stacked one above another on a pole. The cars were ready to spring forward the instant the lights changed.

Hang On!
Some drag cars can reach 300 miles per hour (483 kph) in just a few seconds.

Car Comparison
A Ferrari can reach 60 miles per hour (100 kph) in 2 seconds.

Safety First
A drag-car driver wears a fireproof suit, a crash helmet, and a neck brace to help prevent injury.

One of the Christmas tree's lights winked on, then another. A third flashed green, and the two cars rocketed forward. Blink and you would miss the race! In just seconds, the cars screamed past the finish line. Having reached 150 miles per hour (240 kph), they were traveling twice as fast as a car on a highway.

Drag racers are often fitted with a parachute to help them stop. It is kept in a small compartment behind the driver's seat.

The drivers released parachutes to help slow the cars. The race was so close that it was hard for the excited crowd to see which car had come in first. Fortunately, the electronic timer caught it all. The winner, in the left-hand lane, was seven-hundredths of a second faster!

The drivers steered over to the road that led the loser from the racing lanes and the winner to his next race. Both drivers were handed a small ticket that noted the time of their run and their final speed.

For the rest of the day, the winning car beat every competitor it met. After two hours, the driver had won seven races. He had been racing for less than a minute in all.

Not So Quick
Drag bikes are slower than drag cars. They have to be to avoid rearing up and doing wheelies. That would slow them down even more!

Slower Still
Drag trucks are even slower than drag bikes. Because of their size, they take twice as long as a drag car to tear down a quarter-mile (400-m) strip.

Getting Dizzy
Le Mans cars follow a circuit that is about 8 miles (13 km) long. They'll lap the circuit some 350 times during the race.

Running Start
Drivers used to start Le Mans by running across the track and jumping into their cars. This no longer happens because it is very dangerous.

LE MANS

One of the world's most famous endurance races is held every year close to Le Mans, a town in France.

The town comes alive each May and June when dozens of powerful cars and thousands of excited spectators arrive. The cars have come to take part in a grueling 24-hour-long race around a long circuit near the town. It's fast, it's tiring, and it's thrilling!

In fact, although they only drive around an 8-mile (13-km) circuit, by the end of Le Mans the cars have covered about 3,000 miles (4,800 km). It's the same as crossing the United States—and then coming a part of the way back!

Wet or Dry?
Grooved tires are used if it rains, smooth slicks if it's dry.

On the day of the race, 70 to 80 cars pull away from the starting line. It's an incredible sight. Round and round the cars roar, circling the course in the time it takes to boil an egg. Each car has a team of three drivers who change places after 15 circuits. That's just over an hour of driving each time.

Used Once
Windshields usually last one race only: they are badly damaged in the 24 hours.

The drivers need to stay as fresh as possible. If they get tired, it's easy to crash. That's why all Le Mans cars must have a towing eye on the front and back. The eye is used to tow them off the track if they crash.

Low = Fast
Le Mans cars are low, at just over 3 feet (1 m) high and wide. This helps them to hug the track, even at high speeds.

Quick Change

A Le Mans car can be jacked up in seconds, raising the car 6 inches (15 cm). Each wheel is held on with just one nut. Tires are changed in the time it takes to tie a shoelace.

Who's That?

Racing machines always have numbers so they can be easily identified.

The best place to watch Le Mans is from the grandstands close to the pits—the areas where the cars are serviced. Cars regularly limp into the pits, thirsty for fuel and urgently needing a new set of tires.

Mechanics swarm around a car like bees the moment it rolls to a stop. Each mechanic has a small task that has been repeatedly rehearsed. Within seconds, the car is refueled, fitted with fresh tires, and speeding away.

AVANTI 3

Tough Truck
This truck competed in an endurance race called the Baja 1000. It covers 620 miles (1,000 km) in Mexico, over rocky and sandy ground.

The pits are busy, not only with cars, resting drivers, and mechanics, but also with photographers and reporters. Behind the pits, each team has a huge garage with mountains of spare parts for the cars.

Drivers have to be careful when they leave the pits. Cold tires don't grip as well as hot tires, and the cars may skid if they pull away too fast. It's a tricky race. That's why, in 2021, of the 61 cars that left the starting line, a smaller number, 44, made it to the finish line.

Engine Power
Le Mans cars are fitted with engines that have four times the muscle of ordinary cars! Most engines are positioned behind the driver—not in front as in a family car.

THRUST SSC

Thrust SSC (the initials stand for SuperSonic Car) was built to take the world land speed record. It was also the first car to go supersonic, or faster than the speed of sound (sound travels at about 760 miles per hour [1,223 kph]). But the team of people who built the car almost didn't make an attempt at the speed record.

The car was built in Britain, but it needed a long, flat stretch of ground to attempt a speed trial. Nowhere in Britain was suitable.

Fast Track
Thrust SSC is designed to cut through the air as neatly as possible. It is long, thin, and hugs the ground. This aerodynamic shape helps it to go faster.

However, Black Rock Desert in Nevada in the United States was ideal. The desert is long, and its surface is smooth. The problem was that the team couldn't afford to buy fuel for the airplane they needed to fly the car over.

Then, someone suggested they ask people to donate money to buy 25-gallon (95-liter) amounts of jet fuel. After an appeal on the Internet and publicity in newspapers, money began to pour in. The team soon had what they needed. They were set to go for the record.

Slow Start
The first land speed record was set in 1898 by Gaston de Chasseloup-Laubat. His final speed was 39 mph (63 kph). Today, a bicycle racer beats this!

Old Record
The previous land speed record holder, *Thrust 2*, took the record in 1983 at 633.468 miles per hour (1,019 kph).

A Speedy Car
The Hennessey Venom F5, the fastest street-legal car in the world, can get up to 311 miles per hour (500 kph).

A Speedy Truck
The world's fastest pickup truck is the Banks Sidewinder. It set a record when it reached 222 miles per hour (357 kph).

October 15, 1997, was a perfect autumn day. It was perfect weather, too, for trying to set a new speed record. As Andy Green, driver of the *Thrust SSC*, eased open the throttle, the giant black car began to roll. It moved slowly at first so its jets didn't inhale desert dust. As it picked up speed, the afterburners began to blaze and poke their 40-foot- (12-m-) long tongues of flame out behind the engines. It was an amazing sight.

The driver sat so low he could only see 2 miles (3 km) ahead. To keep on course, he followed a white line of gypsum powder the team had sprinkled on the desert floor.

Halfway along the track was the measured mile (1.6 km). By the time the car got there, it was traveling at 763 miles per hour (1,228 kph). That's slightly faster than the speed of sound. It zipped through in under five seconds.

Onlookers saw the 10-ton (9-t) jet car slip past as steady as a train, chased by a 300-foot- (90-m-) wide carpet of desert dust lifted by the trailing shock wave. A few seconds later the double crack of *Thrust SSC*'s two jet engines breaking the sound barrier split the air.

Two minutes after it set off, the car came to a stop. It was 13 miles (20 km) from where it started. *Thrust SSC* was the proud owner of a new world record.

A Speedy Plane
A *747* crew, flying overhead at the right moment, would have been shocked to see *Thrust SSC* moving faster than it was flying.

Catching Up
Thrust SSC broke the sound barrier on the ground exactly 50 years after the first plane, the X-1, did so in the air.

Fastest Person
The fastest person in the world runs 110 yards (100 m) in just under 10 seconds. That's about 27 miles an hour (43 kph).

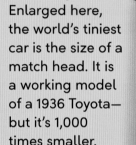

Think Tiny
Enlarged here, the world's tiniest car is the size of a match head. It is a working model of a 1936 Toyota—but it's 1,000 times smaller.

Think Bigger
One of the smallest cars you may spot is the Smart car from Daimler Benz. Two will fit into a normal-size parking space.

STRETCH LIMOUSINE

In 1986, the first thing a lottery winner did with his prize was to buy the best Cadillac he could. Then he told friends he was going to cut it in half. He wanted a stretch limousine—and that is how they are made!

The car was sent to a special limo-building factory. The owner asked for a super stretch limo. The factory would open the car up and lengthen the body by 10 feet (3 m).

The owner called the car American Dream. Ten people could fit inside, and it was the longest car in the world. Its features included a jacuzzi, king-size waterbed, helipad, putting green, and swimming pool.

Over time, the limo fell into disrepair. But after restoring it—and lengthening the car by a fraction of an inch—the limo's new owner set a new world record. American Dream is now 100 feet 1.50 inches (30.54 m) long. It has 46 wheels along with a new pool, putting green, and helipad. Up to 75 people can fit inside. In the future, they might even make it longer!

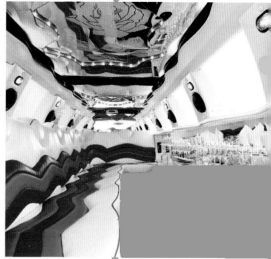

All Jazzed Up
Limousines are usually luxuriously fitted inside. Neon lights and painted ceilings add to the glamor.

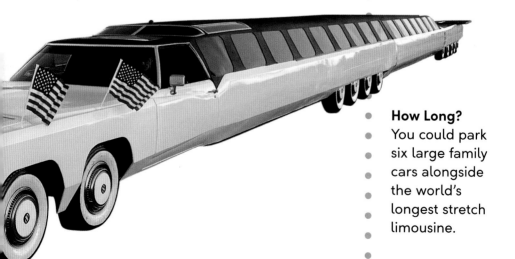

How Long?
You could park six large family cars alongside the world's longest stretch limousine.

DEEP-SEA SUBMERSIBLE

Two scientists and a pilot climbed down into *Alvin*, a deep-sea submersible. The hatches clanged shut. Then a crane lifted the little craft over the ship's side and gently set it down on the waves.

Getting Dark
There is no light 3,000 feet (900 m) below sea level. Submersibles depend on powerful lights if they are going deeper.

Going Down
Scuba divers can only dive to 160 feet (50 m). In an atmospheric diving suit, a diver can go to 10 times that depth.

Once in the water, *Alvin* is stable enough for a person to stand on its top.

The 23-foot- (7-m-) long diving vessel bobbed on the swell and then dipped underwater. Now it moved more like a spaceship than a seagoing ship as it gracefully began to sink. Its journey would take it down almost 2.8 miles (4.5 km) into the inky black ocean depths. The descent would take over two hours.

Alvin's crew was glad to be wearing thermal underwear and heavy sweaters. The water outside was icy cold and that affected the temperature inside. As they huddled in the tiny cabin, only one light was kept on to save power. It was eerily quiet, though the crew did keep in regular contact with the ship above through a cordless telephone.

As it neared the seafloor, Alvin halted and the pilot flipped on a bank of powerful lights. The crew peered out of Alvin's portholes. What would they see?

Going Deeper
In the deepest parts of the sea, water pressure is 1,000 times greater than at the surface. Normal submarines cannot go this deep—the pressure would flatten them.

On Camera
In 1986, Alvin snapped photos of the wreckage of the RMS Titanic in the North Atlantic Ocean. The Titanic sank on April 15, 1912.

Deeper Still
In 2019, explorer Victor Vescovo made a solo dive to Challenger Deep in the Mariana Trench, Earth's lowest known point. He reached 35,876 feet (10,935 m) in the submersible *Limiting Factor*. Vescovo went deeper than filmmaker James Cameron, who made the first solo dive to Challenger Deep in the submersible *Deepsea Challenger* in 2012.

Pioneers of the Deep
In 1960, Don Walsh and Jacques Piccard were the first people to reach the bottom of the Challenger Deep, in a submersible called the *Trieste*.

Skyscrapers of black rock loomed out of the dark. Nearby were the smoking hot-water vents the scientists had come to study. Heated by volcanic rocks deep in the earth, water gushed out of the vents at temperatures hot enough to melt lead. Yet small plants and animals lived around the vents. The scientists were surprised. They had not expected to find so much life living in such an extreme environment.

The pilot brought *Alvin* closer. The machine's two big robotic arms swung down to collect samples of the gushing water. The scientists knew this would stink like rotten eggs. Then *Alvin* moved away to settle on the seabed where the scientists could gather further samples.

After four hours, the work was complete. The craft and its crew began the two-hour journey back to the surface. *Alvin* had forever changed scientists' understanding of where life could exist.

OFFSHORE POWERBOATS

Each year from June to November, powerboat crews from all over Europe and the Middle East gather for a season of races. In open seas, they battle to win the World Championships of offshore powerboat racing.

Offshore powerboats are huge. They weigh the same as five family cars and stretch a good 43 feet (13 m). Their massive twin hulls, called catamarans, are made out of two space-age materials— carbon fiber and Kevlar.

What's That?
This odd-looking racing machine is a swamp buggy. It is raced through muddy swamps in Florida, USA. Swamp buggies were originally built as hunting machines.

The combination is lighter than steel but a lot tougher. Into the hulls go two fighter-plane cockpits—one for the driver and one for the throttler.

The two crew members are strapped into their seats for safety. Both wear life jackets and crash helmets, and each has an air supply. They talk to each other, and to team members on shore, through intercoms in their helmets.

The intercoms are vital pieces of equipment. Once a race begins, the roar of the engines means the crew cannot hear each other without them.

Skirted Boats
Tiny hovercraft race at 85 miles per hour (137 kph) every year at the World Championships in France. They follow a water-and-wet-grass circuit.

One or Two?
Offshore powerboats used to have single hulls and open cockpits. Today's twin-hulled boats, with their closed canopies, are much safer.

Boats jostle for position when a race begins, narrowly avoiding hitting each other. The race course is marked with anchored floats called buoys. The boats have to maneuver around them.

Inside each boat, the driver begins checking the navigation system and compass to stay on course. The throttler watches the wind and waves, trying to guess what the boat will do next.

Running into the wind can speed a boat up, as it lifts the hull out of the water. However, if the boat rises off the top of a wave to fly through the air, the throttle is hauled back. This stops the propeller from spinning too fast and breaking!

The throttler's adjustments can mean the extra mile (km) per hour that will win the race. But at speeds of 150 miles per hour (240 kph), the throttler's moves have to be instant!

Slow Down!
Choppy seas can slow a powerboat by 50 miles per hour (80 kph) or more.

Jet Boats
In New Zealand, small jet boats are raced up shallow rivers. They have no propeller to catch on the bottom.

Formula 1 Boats
These racing boats are fast and furious. They seat one person, and, like offshore powerboats, are twin-hulled. They can speed up from 0 to 100 miles per hour (160 kph) in five seconds.

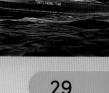

HYDROPLANE RACING

Hydroplane racing is the fastest and most dangerous of all watersports. On a 2.5-mile (4-km) course, the boats shoot down the straight stretches at 200 miles per hour (320 kph) and take corners at 160 miles per hour (250 kph). It's thrilling to watch.

The hulls barely touch the water. Hydroplanes basically travel on a cushion of air. But the boats shake violently, pounding over the surface of the water like hammers.

The violent motion can temporarily blur the driver's eyesight! Yet over a 20-minute race, drivers must tweak the controls to keep their boat as high out of the water as possible. At the same time, they try to overtake other hydroplanes. That's not as easy as it sounds.

A boat that overtakes must not cut in front of the other boat until it is more than five boat-lengths ahead. That's because each boat creates a huge "rooster"-tail of spray that flings a ton of water into the air. If this pelted down in the path of a following boat, it would flood the cushion of air the boat was riding on. When this happens, it forces the following boat up and over in a spectacular somersault.

Power Crazy
A hydroplane is ridiculously powerful. Its engine is actually four times more powerful than a Formula 1 car engine.

No Protection
Hydroplanes used to have open cockpits. But increasing speeds led to more accidents, and today's drivers sit in sealed cockpits.

A hydroplane is cleverly designed, with a double front hull but a single rear hull. As it picks up speed, its two front hulls become airborne. This means it doesn't have a huge weight of water to move aside. With only the back hull and propeller dragging in the water, most of its power turns straight into speed.

The secret of hydroplane racing, though, is what the boats use to push themselves along with. They are fitted with a giant helicopter engine.

The engine is fine-tuned to produce an incredible 4,200 horsepower. That's enough power to run 42 good-size family cars!

The engines do their job, but the speed puts lives in danger. In the past, hydroplaning has killed many drivers. That's why today's drivers sit cocooned in a sealed cockpit fitted with escape hatches and an oxygen supply. Accidents still happen with these speed monsters, but nowadays drivers usually survive.

Fuel Up
Many hydroplane engines run on alcohol, gas, or other kinds of fuel. These give more power than the gasoline used in cars.

Mi-26 HELICOPTER

The twin engines coughed and belched smoke as one of the world's largest helicopters, Russia's *Mi-26*, started up. The noise was tremendous.

Moments later, the helicopter's eight rotor blades began to whisk the air, stirring up the dust beneath. They gathered speed and merged into a whirring disk that was wide enough to park ten lanes of cars beneath it.

At last, with a great clatter, the mammoth helicopter shrugged once and heaved itself into the air. It was on an emergency mission in the Ural Mountains of Russia, where a series of forest fires raged. The fires had already charred huge areas of forest. They were now nearing roads and villages.

Next in Line
After the *Mi-26*, the next biggest helicopter is the *CH-53K King Stallion*.

Smallest of All
There's only room for one in the world's smallest helicopter. In fact it only weighs as much as a small adult.

The five-person crew of the *Mi-26* had scrambled into the air minutes after the call came through. Their job was to ferry firefighters to the scene of the blaze.

That's why 78 firefighters were now crammed together on the helicopter's cargo deck. Each was fitted out with a parachute and a large pack of firefighting equipment. They were ready for the drop and the task ahead of them.

In the Air
In 1939, a Russian engineer named Sikorsky, living in the U.S., built the first working single-rotor helicopter.

1,500 Years Ago
The idea behind a helicopter is more than 1,500 years old. Back then, the Chinese had a toy called a flying top that used feathered rotors to fly.

Back and Forth
A helicopter's rotor blades tilt in two directions so a helicopter can fly forward and backward.

As they reached the fires, the helicopter crew could see a wall of smoke. They could not see through it, but several miles (kms) west of the smoke line the pilot spotted a winding logging road. This was their drop zone. The tree-lined road was too narrow to set the *Mi-26* down, so the pilot hovered at about 1,500 feet (450 m) while the crew lowered the cargo deck's rear hatch.

In waves, the firefighters dived headlong out of the helicopter. Parachutes snapped open and they drifted down onto the road. Ten minutes later, all 78 men were safely on the ground and the crew was raising the hatch.

The giant helicopter dipped its nose and headed back to base to collect more firefighters.

THE *X-15*

The giant *B-52* bomber rumbled down the runway and lifted off. It carried no bombs. Instead, a small black dart was tucked under its right wing like a rolled-up newspaper.

The dart was an *X-15*, a U.S. Air Force experiment to see if it was possible to fly an occupied plane into space. By hitching a ride on the *B-52*, the *X-15* halved the fuel it needed to get airborne. It carried one pilot and was basically a flying fuel tank. It had stubby wings on the side and a rocket engine on its back.

The *X-15* was the fifteenth in a line of experimental aircraft that began with the *X-1*.

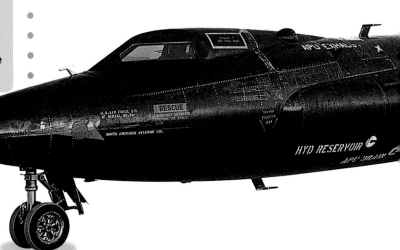

The original goal of these planes was to go higher than 19 miles (30 km) and faster than three times the speed of sound. The X-15 achieved this, and more. It was the first plane ever to fly into space. And it broke all records for being the highest, fastest, and most dangerous way to fly.

Suddenly, the X-15 left the B-52. Its engine fired, and it climbed straight up as if aiming to punch a hole in the sky. By the time it reached 37 miles (60 km), there was so little air left that its wings had nothing to bite into anymore.

X-1
The X-1 was the first plane to fly faster than the speed of sound.

Wrong Engine
If the X-15 had been fitted with a jet engine, it would have spluttered and died long before reaching space. A jet engine needs air, and there is no air in space.

The X-15 had skids instead of rear wheels.

It now used a dozen tiny rockets to steer itself. Up and up it climbed. By the time it was out of fuel, it was over 67 miles (100 km) up. The pilot could see the curve of the planet and look down on the atmosphere.

There is no clear line where the atmosphere ends and space begins. Most people in space exploration agree that it happens at about 50 miles (80 km) up. That's why this pilot, and half his colleagues, earned themselves the right to wear astronaut wings. For at the top of its flight, the *X-15* was traveling like a spaceship.

Low Fliers
High-flying passenger jets cruise around the world at a height of about 7.5 miles (12 km). The *X-15* went nine times higher.

66672

U.S. AIR

USAF

FUEL VENT

By now, the X-15 was rocketing along at about 4,500 miles per hour (7,200 kph). That's just over six times the speed of sound. At normal highway speeds, a car would have to travel nonstop for three days and nights to go as far as the X-15 would have done had it kept this up for an hour.

Turning back to Earth, the plane glided down. It was a strange sight. To save weight, it had no rear wheels, only a pair of metal skids—a bit like gigantic skis. After landing, it simply skied along the ground until it stopped. The flight had taken just over 10 minutes.

Hot Stuff
At six times the speed of sound, the X-15's skin got very hot, reaching a scorching 1,202°F (650°C). It had a special metal surface to withstand this.

Short But Speedy
Each X-15 flight lasted about 10 minutes.

IDEAS FOR THE FUTURE

Flying car

Ideas for machines of the future may sound odd. But a space rocket probably sounded unusual to people one hundred years ago, too!

Can you imagine being able to drive through the skies, at eye level with skyscrapers and soaring birds? Some car and aviation companies are imagining just that.

They are racing to see who can perfect the world's first flying car. More than a dozen are in development. The first sky-high cars will likely be taxis that can transport more than one person at a time.

On water, the *Airfish 8* is a boat dressed up like a plane. It is powered by a car engine and uses high-octane unleaded gasoline.

The 56.5-ft- (17.2-m-) long craft is operated by two crew members. It travels three times faster than other boats. Designed to fly just above the waves, it provides a smooth ride for the six to eight passengers inside.

New ideas are reshaping vehicles on land, too, particularly in how automobiles are powered. The goal is to use renewable resources. Solar energy isn't reliable on cloudy days, so most new automobiles use a combination of solar power and electricity.

One model, Aptera, can travel up to 40 miles (64.4 km) a day on solar power alone. Combining that with electricity, the car can travel up to 1,000 miles (1,609 km) before it needs to be recharged.

Water Flight
As the *Airfish 8* speeds up, it rises in the water. Flying up to 122 mph (196 kph), it could revolutionize the way people travel across the sea.

Conserving Energy
Aptera seats two people. Its aerodynamic design and lightweight materials make it more fuel efficient.

Flying Supersonic
The first supersonic passenger jet was the Concorde, which was retired in 2003. Its long, pointed nose lowered for landing and takeoff.

Speed Monsters
Supersonic planes of the future will be more than twice as long as the Concorde!

There are exciting plans for future high-speed air travel as well. Designers are hard at work on a 50-seat jet airplane that flies at up to 3,800 miles per hour (6,200 kph). That's about seven times as fast as a regular commercial airliner.

This new plane, which breaks the speed of sound, is called a supersonic airplane. It could travel from the United States to Japan in less than three hours. Right now, the trip between the two countries takes about four times as long!

Want to travel even higher? Scientists are working on technology for an elevator that can take people to space.

A material called graphene, which is 200 times stronger than steel, could be used to secure the elevator to Earth. With the push of a button, space tourists and astronauts alike could skim the stars!

The possibilities for machines of the future are fascinating. What do you think extreme machines will look like?

An Updated Idea
The idea for a space elevator is not new. A Russian scientist first proposed one in 1895.

GLOSSARY

Aerodynamic
The smooth, streamlined shape that helps a car or airplane slip through air easily

Circuit
A set course around which machines can race

Drag racer
The name given to cars and motorbikes that race short distances in a straight line

Endurance race
A race run over a long distance which takes a long time

Fuel
The material that powers an engine to make it go

Gears
These control the speed of an engine

Glider
An airplane that flies without any engine power

Horsepower
A means of measuring an engine's power

Hull
The part of a boat that sits in the water

Hydroplane
A fast motorboat that skims over the water with most of its hull in the air

Jet engine
All engines run on two things: fuel and oxygen. Jet engines gulp their oxygen from air.

Rocket engine
A rocket engine carries the oxygen it needs in a tank called an oxidizer

Rotor
The whirling blades above a helicopter are known as rotors because of the way they spin. Each rotor is a mini-wing that lifts as it rotates.

Shock wave
Anything going faster than the speed of sound creates a shock wave in the air. We hear it as a loud bang. It can shatter glass at close range.

Speed of sound
Sound moves much slower than light—that's why you see lightning before you hear it.

Submersible
A submarine cruises underwater as well as dives and climbs. A submersible mainly just dives and climbs.

Throttle
The control handle or pedal that feeds fuel to an engine. As it is opened, more fuel is pumped in and the engine speeds up. To slow down, the throttle has to be closed.

INDEX

QUIZ

Answer the questions to see what you have learned. Check your answers in the key below.

1. What does a drag-car driver release to help slow the car?

2. How many drivers make up a team in the Le Mans car race?

3. What world record did *Thrust* SSC accomplish?

4. What did the scientists aboard *Alvin*, a submersible, hope to learn?

5. What was the name of the first plane to fly into space?

6. True or False: Scientists are working on technology for a space elevator.

7. What is the name of the boat that is three times faster than other boats?

8. How do members of a powerboat team talk to each other?

1. A parachute 2. Three 3. It broke the world land speed record
4. About the plants and animals that lived in the deep sea 5. The *X-15*
6. True 7. *Airfish 8* 8. Through intercoms in their helmets